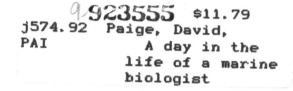

A DAY IN THE LIFE OF A
Marine Biologist

by David Paige
photography by Roger Ruhlin

Troll Associates

Library of Congress Catalog Card Number: 80-54097
ISBN 0-89375-446-3   ISBN 0-89375-447-1 Paper Edition

The author and publisher wish to thank the Rosenstiel School of Marine and Atmospheric Science, University of
Miami; marine scientists Lynn Walter, Lise Dowd, Tim Bently, Kim Harrison, and Dana Kent; divemaster Stu
McCormick; Jean Yehle; and the Miami Seaquarium for their generous cooperation and assistance.

Photography credits: p. 26,—Stephen Sanacore, p. 27—Animals, Animals/Oxford Scientific Films

10 9 8 7 6 5 4 3 2

Early in the morning, Lynn Walter is already at work as a marine biologist. Her first job of the day is to collect shellfish, crayfish, and worms in a muddy swamp. For this kind of work, she wears a sweatshirt and shorts. For her other duties, she may wear a shirt and jeans, a lab coat, or even a diver's wetsuit.

Lynn works at an oceanographic institute where
marine biologists study ocean life. Her special research project concerns sea turtles. This one, a
loggerhead turtle that weighs almost as much as
Lynn, has been refusing to eat. Perhaps the live food
Lynn has gathered in the swamp will be to the
turtle's liking.

Although she suspects the turtle is simply tired of eating the same thing day after day, Lynn checks for signs of illness. With the help of another scientist, she pulls the turtle to the surface of the tank. It seems active enough. Lynn feels certain that a change in diet will start the turtle eating again.

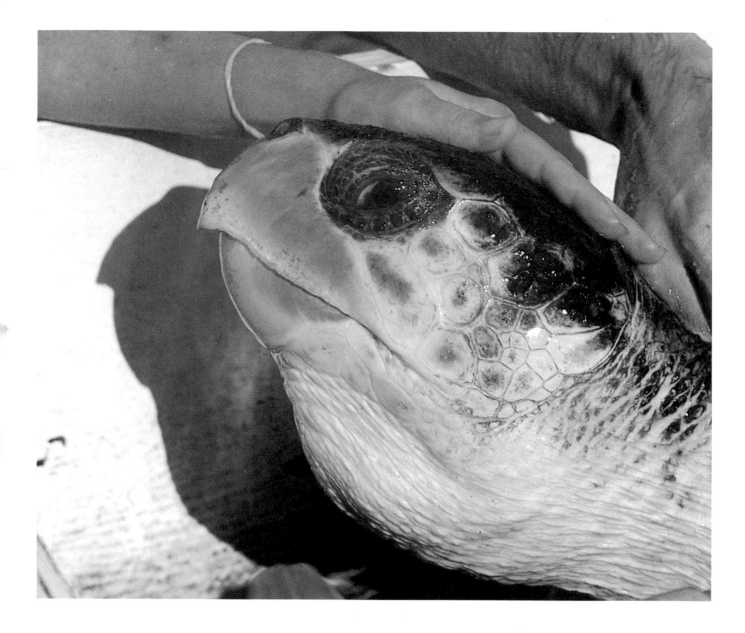

A loggerhead's sharp beak is strong enough to crack open hard-shelled clams and other shellfish. If angered, a sea turtle uses its beak as a weapon. Lynn has learned to be careful around animals, and to treat them gently.

Some animals are too dangerous to handle at all. Though the sharks in this outdoor pool have been sluggish, the scientists cannot get close to check them. They lower a chunk of raw tuna on a rope, to see how well the sharks are eating. This one's appetite seems normal. Lynn will check them again tomorrow.

All the marine biologists take turns caring for the fish and other animals in the institute's aquarium tanks. These Sheepshead minnows are nibbling a cube of frozen brine shrimp. Lynn keeps a chart of how well they eat, how they behave at feeding time, and whether they show any signs of illness.

Later, Lynn and a co-worker examine a new arrival at the institute. All new arrivals are checked carefully. This freshwater prawn is from a river in Southeast Asia. A prawn is a kind of shellfish. This one is missing a leg, which was broken off during the long journey. But prawns can easily grow new legs.

Now that feeding time is over, Lynn can work on her own research project. She uses smaller, green turtles because they are easier to handle than loggerhead turtles. About half Lynn's time is spent in the laboratory, working on her project. She is part of a team that is trying to answer a puzzling question about sea turtles.

Although they must breathe air like other turtles, sea turtles are able to stay underwater for many hours at a time. Sometimes they stay submerged for several days. The air in their lungs cannot possibly last that long. Do sea turtles have some other way to store oxygen when they dive?

The answer may require years of tests and experiments. Some tests are routine. An electrocardiograph machine prints out a graph of the sea turtle's heartbeat. Then a balloon is placed over the turtle's face as it breathes. A respiration machine attached to the balloon measures how much air is inhaled and exhaled with each breath.

A blood sample is taken, and the amount of oxygen in the turtle's blood is measured. All these tests are done when the animal is out of the water. Later, after the turtle has been submerged for many hours, each test will be repeated. The results of the two sets of tests can then be compared and analyzed.

When the sea turtle is back in its tank, Lynn puts a clean lab coat on over her work clothes. It is impossible to collect swamp creatures and carry turtles without getting dirty, yet she must not risk soiling any of the samples to be tested.

By looking at a thin smear of blood through a micro-scope, Lynn can count the number of red blood cells in the sample. Water from the turtle's tank is also analyzed. But so far, the scientists on the team have no clues to how the sea turtles can stay underwater for as long as they do.

Lynn hopes to be able to find out more by studying sea turtles in their natural habitat, thousands of miles out in the ocean. She plans to go on a two-month trip to the Galapagos Islands with other marine biologists next summer. Now she helps the supervisor of the expedition plot the voyage on ocean charts.

This ocean-going ship will take the team through the Panama Canal to the Pacific Ocean, then southwest to the equator. Lynn has never been on so long a voyage. Every time she goes to the dock, she looks at the research ship and wonders what adventures lie ahead of her.

The ship has huge winches and pulleys to raise and lower scientific equipment weighing several tons. The winch also hauls in enormous nets used for collecting specimens. Lynn imagines the excitement of hauling in a giant sea turtle twice the size of the large one she fed this morning.

But now, Lynn must stop daydreaming, for there are chores to be done at the dock. Again, fresh food must be gathered. This time it is plankton—tiny plants and animals that float in the ocean. Cone-shaped nets are lowered into the water to gather them.

The ocean current flows through the nets, carrying large numbers of plankton. All kinds of plankton will be captured, from thread-sized worms and miniature sea horses to hundreds of thousands of creatures that can only be seen under a microscope.

The plankton is harvested in jars attached to the ends of the nets. This haul has a special surprise—a comb jelly. This tiny animal looks like a mushy ice cube, and is so clear that Lynn can see right through it. Comb jellies feed on plankton. So do thousands of other ocean animals, including the largest animal of all, the blue whale.

This afternoon, Lynn will be going to sea on the institute's smaller vessel, the *Orca*. She will be collecting samples of marine life from a polluted area nearby. Helping out on this project will give Lynn a chance to practice her scuba diving. She reads the charts to understand exactly where she will dive.

As the boat pulls away from the dock, Lynn begins to check her equipment. She may dive very deep, and stay under the water for as long as thirty minutes. She must be able to rely totally on her equipment. The dial on her tank tells her the air regulator is working properly.

Lynn gets into a short wetsuit. If the water were cold, she would need a long wetsuit—one that covers her legs. She needs help getting into her buoyancy compensator. This is a yellow vest that automatically inflates or deflates, so Lynn can "float" at whatever depth she wishes.

By the time Lynn has all her gear on, the boat has reached its destination. She steps down the ladder into the water, carrying her flippers and a net specimen bag. Jumping in could damage her equipment, and flippers could get caught in the ladder. So she puts her flippers on after she is in the water.

When Lynn is ready to dive, she will be handed a slurp gun, which she will use to collect specimens. The gun is not a weapon. Instead, it sucks fish toward it, so they can be netted in the specimen bag. This way, the fish are not injured.

Whenever Lynn scuba dives, she must be on the lookout for danger. The greatest danger in these waters is the Portuguese man-of-war. This very large jellyfish paralyzes its prey with poisonous tentacles that may grow as long as forty feet. Any diver that brushes against them might be paralyzed.

By the time Lynn climbs back on board the boat, she
has filled her specimen bag with fish, and has
gathered several samples of bottom mud. Later, the
mud samples will be checked for signs of pollution.
The specimens of undersea life, however, are exam-
ined immediately.

Some fish are put into holding tanks to keep them alive. Others are put into specimen jars. This fish is a jack—a species that is often caught in these waters and eaten. Fish that are eaten must be free of dangerous chemicals and poisons. Tests will determine whether the jacks in this area are safe to eat.

Back at the dock, Lynn prepares to go ashore. The specimen jar has been labeled with the time, date, and exact location at which the fish were collected. Hundreds of specimens, collected from many places all during the year, give marine biologists an idea of how bad the pollution problem has become.

An autopsy will be performed on this fish. Blood, muscle, fat, and internal organs will be tested for dangerous chemicals. If the amounts are high, people in the fishing industry will be warned. But an autopsy will take several hours, so it will have to wait until tomorrow. Lynn and the others prepare to leave for the day.

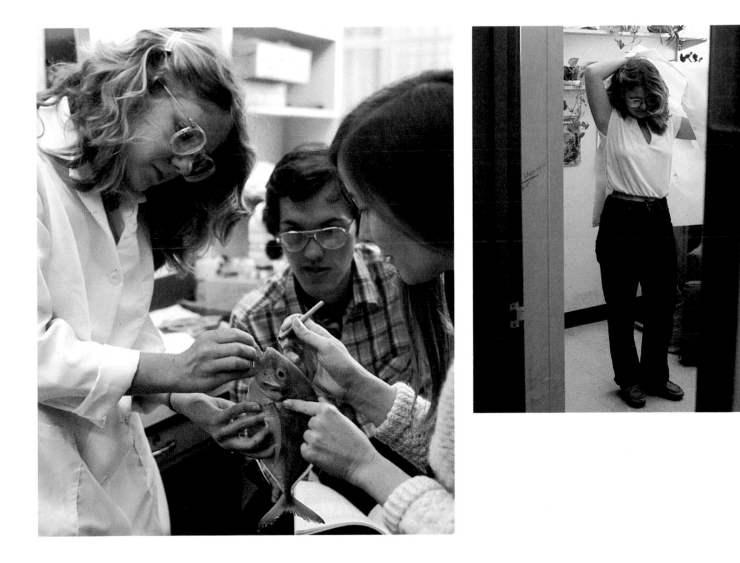

The institute is closing for the night. Lynn has had a pleasant morning, working with the animals in the laboratory. She has enjoyed her afternoon, working in the outdoor laboratory shared by all marine biologists—the open ocean. A picnic on the beach is a perfect ending for a day that has been busy as well as rewarding.